3 6653 00166 8239

11/07

Florida Manatees

Warm Water Miracles

by Meish Goldish

Consultants:
Nicole Adimey, Biologist, U.S. Fish and Wildlife Service

Dr. Thomas R. Reinert, Marine Mammal Program
Florida Fish and Wildlife Conservation Commission

BEARPORT
PUBLISHING

New York, New York

Credits

Cover and Title Page, © Doug Perrine/SeaPics.com; 4, © George Skene/Orlando Sentinel/ MCT/Newscom.com; 5, © Doug Perrine/SeaPics.com; 6, Florida Photo Collection/ Florida State Archives; 7, © Todd Pusser/naturepl.com; 8, © Science Photo Library/Photo Researchers, Inc.; 9, © Pölzer/f1 online/Alamy; 10, © David Schrichte/SeaPics.com; 11L, © David Schrichte/SeaPics.com; 11R, © Doug Perrine/naturepl.com; 12, © Paul Wayne Wilson/ PhotoStockFile/Alamy; 13, © Dan Burton/naturepl.com; 14, Katherine Brill, Marine Mammal Pathobiology Lab, Florida Fish and Wildlife Conservation Commission; 15L, © Kevin Fleming/ Corbis; 15R, © Bruce R. Bennett/ZUMA Press/Newscom.com; 16L, © Jeff Greenberg/ Indexstock; 16R, © Marty Snyderman; 17, © AP Images/Daytona Beach News-Journal, Craig Litten; 19L, © Visual&Written/Newscom.com; 19R, © Stephen M. Dowell/Orlando Sentinel/ MCT/Newscom.com; 20, © Doug Perrine/SeaPics.com; 21, © Fred Whitehead/Animals Animals-Earth Scenes; 22, South Florida Museum, Bradenton, Florida; 23, South Florida Museum, Bradenton, Florida; 24, © AP Images/The News-Journal, Brian Myrick; 25, © Doug Perrine/SeaPics.com; 26, © Douglas Faulkner/Photo Researchers, Inc.; 27, © Jurgen Freund/ naturepl.com; 28, © Doug Perrine/naturepl.com; 29T, © Doug Perrine/naturepl.com; 29B, © Masa Ushioda/SeaPics.com; 31, © Rough Guides/Alamy; 32, © Jack Sullivan/Alamy.

Publisher: Kenn Goin
Editorial Director: Adam Siegel
Creative Director: Spencer Brinker
Photo Researcher: Amy Dunleavy
Cover Design: Dawn Beard Creative

Library of Congress Cataloging-in-Publication Data

Goldish, Meish.
  Florida manatees : warm water miracles / by Meish Goldish.
      p. cm. — (America's animal comebacks)
  Includes bibliographical references and index.
  ISBN-13: 978-1-59716-507-5 (lib. bdg.)
  ISBN-10: 1-59716-507-7 (lib. bdg.)
  1. Manatees—Florida—Juvenile literature. I. Title.

QL737.S63G65 2008
599.5509759—dc22

                              2007010311

For more information, write to Bearport Publishing Company, Inc., 101 Fifth Avenue, Suite 6R, New York, New York 10003. Printed in the United States of America.

10 9 8 7 6 5 4 3 2 1

Contents

A Close Call

Police officer Andy Pallen was **patrolling** the waters of south Florida in January of 2007. Suddenly, he saw a motorboat heading toward two manatees—a mother and her **calf**. Pallen waved wildly. He yelled at the driver to stop, but it was too late. The boat hit the mother, scraping her back.

Officers watch for speeding boats in places where Florida manatees live.

Luckily, the **collision** was not deadly. Officer Pallen was thankful. The number of Florida manatees was **estimated** to be only around 3,000. In the last ten years, almost 800 of the gentle sea animals had been killed in boat collisions. Florida had boating laws to protect them. Yet the deadly accidents continued. Was the Florida manatee in danger of dying out?

Boat collisions are a major cause of manatee deaths today.

Manatees live in water but they are **mammals**, not fish. Manatees are closely related to elephants.

Hunted Creatures

Long before motorboats were invented, Florida manatees were struggling to survive. People began hunting these giant sea creatures thousands of years ago. Manatees are easy to catch because they move slowly. They usually swim between two to six miles per hour (3–10 kph).

This drawing from 1896 shows a manatee that was killed for food.

People found many uses for the manatees that they killed. An adult manatee can weigh more than 1,000 pounds (453 kg). So meat from just one animal fed many people. Its skin was made into shoes. Manatee fat was burned as **fuel**. Its bones were used to make medicine and jewelry.

It is hard for manatees to increase their **population** when many of them are killed. Females usually give birth to only one calf about every three years.

A manatee calf drinking its mother's milk

Almost Extinct

By the late 1800s, people had killed so many manatees that they were almost **extinct**. To protect the animals from dying out, in 1893 Florida passed its first law against hunting them. In 1907, a **fine** of $500 was set for killing a manatee.

Steller's sea cow, a relative of the manatee, became extinct from hunting just 27 years after it was discovered in 1741.

The laws that were passed helped the Florida manatee. By the 1970s, the sea creatures were no longer threatened by hunting. Yet the animals were still not safe. A deadly new danger had taken the place of hunters—motorboats.

In 1967, the U.S. government first listed the Florida manatee as an **endangered species**. In 1972, Congress passed the Marine Mammal Protection Act. The law made it **illegal** to hunt, capture, or kill manatees.

Florida manatees live in warm, shallow waters near land, so it was not hard for hunters to find them.

Deadly Boats

From 1950 to 1970, the number of people living in Florida more than doubled. With more people came more motorboats. The drivers often sped in places where manatees swam. Some boaters couldn't see the manatees. The slow-moving animals could not get out of the way in time. Many boaters accidentally hit them.

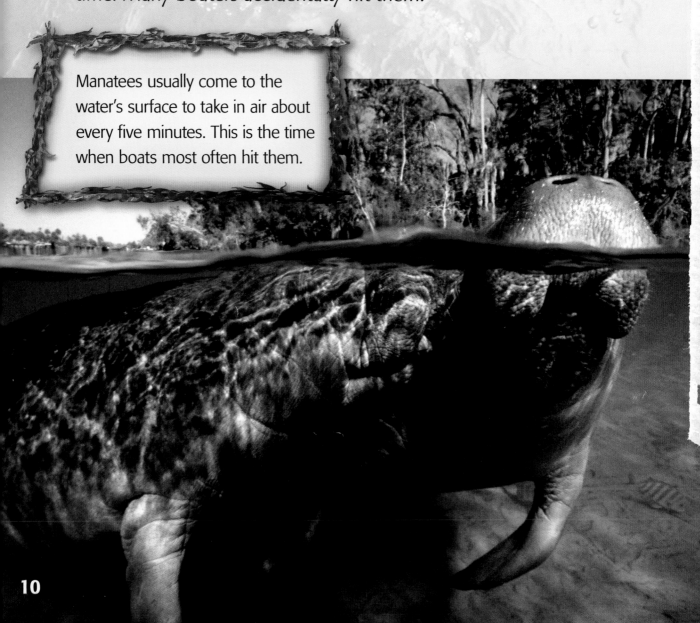

Manatees usually come to the water's surface to take in air about every five minutes. This is the time when boats most often hit them.

Sometimes, manatees were killed instantly in a boat collision. Other times, they were badly hurt. Often, manatees were struck by a boat's **propeller**. The sharp blades made deep cuts and left marks on the animal. Even if the manatee survived, it was often injured for life.

Manatees cannot always get away from boats in time.

Scientists identify many manatees by the scars on their bodies.

Fewer Places to Live

Motorboats weren't the only problem manatees faced from Florida's skyrocketing population. As more people moved to the state, many new homes went up along the **coast**. To make space for them, builders cleared land by cutting down trees.

New homes along Florida's coast have forced manatees to leave the area.

Unfortunately, getting rid of the trees destroyed the manatees' **habitat**. How? There were no longer tree roots to hold down soil. So rain washed lots of dirt and sand into the water where manatees swam. The water turned dark and muddy. As a result, light could no longer reach the sea grass that manatees eat. The plants stopped growing. With less sea grass, it was hard for manatees to live in that part of the water anymore. Their habitat was getting smaller and smaller.

A manatee is called a "sea cow" because it is a large underwater animal that eats sea grass and other plants.

More Dangers

Life was not easy for the manatees. They had to be careful where they swam. If not, they could be killed.

Manatees sometimes got caught in fishing and crab trap lines that were left in the water. Some of the manatees got tangled in them and drowned. Others died after swallowing fishing hooks or garbage that was dumped in the ocean.

This manatee was caught in a crab trap line.

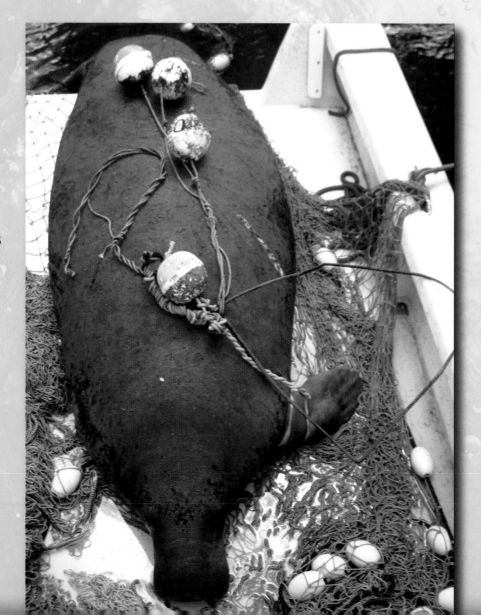

Manatees were also killed by **dams** and **canals**. A dam has underwater doors that control the flow of water. Sometimes, closing doors crushed a manatee to death.

Other manatees died in canals. Their underwater gates raise and lower water for passing boats. Often, manatees got caught in the canal gates and were killed.

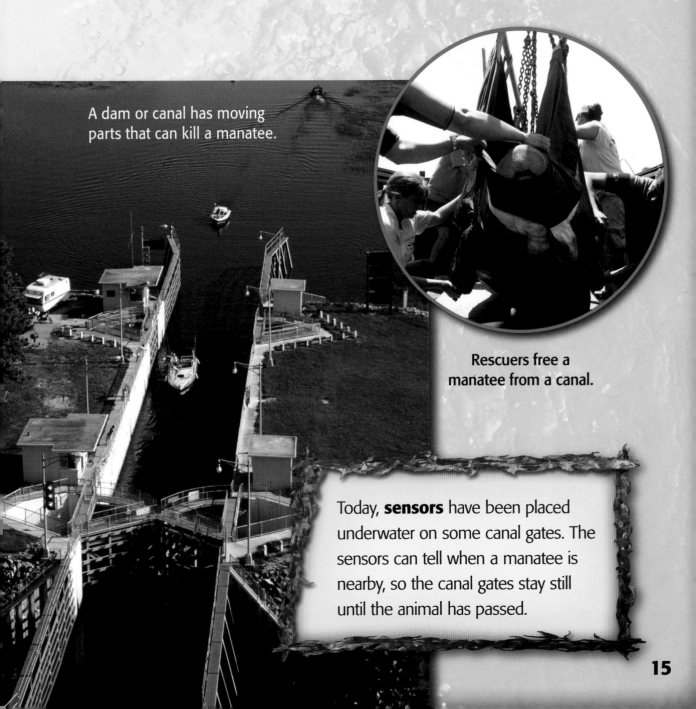

A dam or canal has moving parts that can kill a manatee.

Rescuers free a manatee from a canal.

Today, **sensors** have been placed underwater on some canal gates. The sensors can tell when a manatee is nearby, so the canal gates stay still until the animal has passed.

15

Taking Action

With all the threats facing manatees, the animals needed more protection. So in 1978, **wildlife officials** passed the Florida Manatee **Sanctuary** Act. All of Florida was now declared a safe home for manatees. It was against the law for people to harm them. Anyone doing so could be fined up to $1,000 and spend time in jail.

Signs remind people to watch out for manatees.

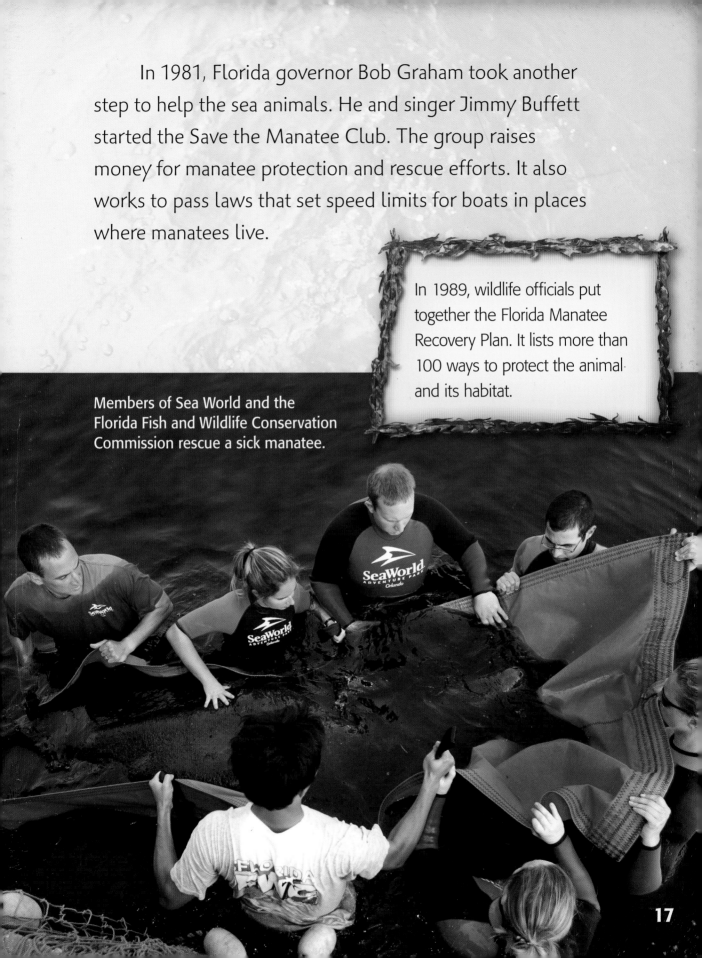

In 1981, Florida governor Bob Graham took another step to help the sea animals. He and singer Jimmy Buffett started the Save the Manatee Club. The group raises money for manatee protection and rescue efforts. It also works to pass laws that set speed limits for boats in places where manatees live.

In 1989, wildlife officials put together the Florida Manatee Recovery Plan. It lists more than 100 ways to protect the animal and its habitat.

Members of Sea World and the Florida Fish and Wildlife Conservation Commission rescue a sick manatee.

Staying Warm

People have worked hard to help the manatee survive. Yet sometimes the animals have been able to solve their own problems.

In the winter, much of Florida's waters turn too cold for manatees. They cannot live in water that is colder than 68°F (20°C) for long periods of time. So the manatees need to find a warm place to live. Where can they go? The gentle sea creatures found a surprising location.

In the winter, manatees stay in warm ocean water around Florida. In the summer, when the ocean becomes warmer, manatees have been seen as far north as Rhode Island.

Florida Manatees in the Wild

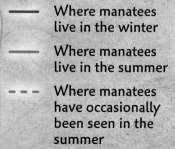

— Where manatees live in the winter

— Where manatees live in the summer

- - - Where manatees have occasionally been seen in the summer

Electric companies use water to cool off the large machines inside their factories. The water gets heated and is then poured back outside. Manatees discovered these warm pools of water. Hundreds of them now gather there during the cold winter months.

Tourists sometimes watch manatees swim in the warm water released by Florida's electric power plants.

Manatees get sick in water that is too cold. The animals stop eating and die.

Safe Homes

People also have helped manatees survive the winter by protecting the animal's habitat. In parts of Florida, warm **spring** water flows throughout the year. Hundreds of manatees come and live in these places during the winter. To protect the animals, some of these areas were turned into **refuges**. Some do not allow motorboats in the winter. Others have slow speed zones.

Blue Spring State Park opened in 1972. Many visitors come to watch the manatees that live there between November and March.

The spring water at Blue Spring State Park is 72°F (22°C) all year round—the perfect temperature for manatees.

Homosassa Springs Wildlife State Park is a refuge for manatees during the winter months. Inside the park, workers and doctors care for injured manatees until they are released back into the wild.

Manatees receive special care at Homosassa Springs.

Manatee Hero

Manatees with safe homes can live long, healthy lives. A good example is Snooty. He is Florida's oldest-living manatee born and raised in **captivity**. Snooty was born in a Miami **aquarium** in 1948. The next year he was moved to a large tank at the South Florida Museum in Bradenton. He still lives there today.

Snooty is one of the most famous manatees in Florida.

Scientists come to the museum to study Snooty. Children and adults learn about manatees by visiting him. Every year, thousands of visitors help Snooty celebrate his birthday. A big party is held at the museum. Children make birthday cards for the manatee. Snooty turned 59 years old in 2007.

Snooty is the first manatee ever to have a recorded date of birth.

Snooty swimming

Keeping Track

People love to watch manatees. Florida wildlife officials like to watch them, too. They began scientifically tracking the manatee population in the early 1990s. Every year they count the animals. In 2007, they counted 2,817 manatees. That number was up from 1,267 in 1991.

This park ranger is keeping track of the number of manatees in Blue Spring State Park.

Wildlife officials fly in planes over Florida to count the number of manatees.

Some people, however, think that there are still not enough manatees. They fear that people might stop caring about the animal's safety. Only time will tell if they are right.

Some people worry that manatees could still die out completely in the future.

The Future

No one knows what the future holds for Florida manatees. Many laws now protect the animals. Yet in the last 10 years, more than 3,000 manatees have died. Around 80 are still killed each year in boating accidents. As more people move to Florida, building and pollution increases. More of the animal's habitat is lost to make room for all the new people.

Manatees are known as "gentle giants" because these large animals never attack anyone.

Even with all these problems, though, there are hopeful signs. Several Florida zoos and aquariums care for ill and injured manatees. Groups such as the Save the Manatee Club give money to protect the animals. Speeding laws help prevent deadly boating accidents. Hopefully, everyone's help will give Florida manatees the bright future they deserve.

Workers at Florida's Sea World keep manatees safe and healthy.

Florida Manatee Facts

In 1973, Congress passed the Endangered Species Act. This law protects animals and plants that are in danger of dying out in the United States. Harmful activities, such as hunting, capturing, collecting, or disturbing endangered species, are illegal under this act.

The Florida manatee was one of the first animals listed under the Endangered Species Act. Here are some other facts about the Florida manatee.

Population: **North American population in 1600:** unknown
North American population today: about 3,000

Weight	Length	Color	Food	Life Span
800–1,200 pounds (363–544 kg)	10–13 feet (3–4 m)	gray or gray-brown	sea grass and other plants	about 50–60 years

Habitat
rivers, bays, and ocean coasts; in winter, both coasts of Florida; in summer, usually as far north as North Carolina, and as far west as Texas

The Florida manatee is one kind of manatee that's making a comeback by increasing its numbers. Other types of manatees are also trying to make a comeback.

Amazonian Manatee

- Amazonian manatees live in the Amazon River in South America. They are the only manatees that live only in fresh water.

- Illegal hunting and habitat destruction are major threats to their survival.

- The current population of Amazonian manatees is not known. It is believed to be between a few hundred and a few thousand.

West African Manatee

- West African manatees live near the coast of western Africa. Their habitat stretches from the countries of Senegal to Angola.

- Illegal hunting and changes to their habitat are the biggest threats to their survival.

- The current population of West African manatees is not known. It is believed to be between a few hundred and a few thousand.

Glossary

aquarium (uh-KWAIR-ee-uhm) a building where people can see many kinds of sea creatures

calf (KAF) a young manatee that needs to drink its mother's milk for food

canals (kuh-NALZ) paths that are made to connect bodies of water so that boats can travel between them

captivity (kap-TIV-uh-tee) a place where an animal lives that is not its natural home and where it cannot travel freely

coast (KOHST) land that runs along an ocean

collision (kuh-LIH-zhuhn) a crash

dams (DAMZ) strong walls built across rivers or streams to hold back water

endangered species (en-DAYN-jurd SPEE-sheez) a kind of animal that is in danger of dying out; no more will be left on Earth

estimated (ESS-ti-*mate*-id) to have figured out the approximate amount of something

extinct (ek-STINGKT) when a kind of plant or animal has died out; no more of its kind is living anywhere on Earth

fine (FINE) money that is paid as a punishment

fuel (FYOO-uhl) something that is used as a source of energy or heat, such as gasoline

habitat (HAB-uh-*tat*) a place in nature where an animal normally lives

illegal (i-LEE-guhl) against the law

mammals (MAM-uhlz) warm-blooded animals that have backbones, hair or fur on their skin, and drink their mothers' milk when they are babies

patrolling (puh-TROHL-ing) traveling around an area to keep it safe

population (*pop*-yuh-LAY-shuhn) the total number of a kind of animal living in a place

propeller (pruh-PEL-ur) spinning blades that make a boat move through water

refuges (REF-yoo-*jiz*) places that protect animals from danger

sanctuary (SANGK-choo-er-ee) an area in nature where animals are protected from being disturbed

sensors (SEN-surz) electronic tools that can tell if something is moving

spring (SPRING) a source of water that flows from the ground

wildlife officials (WILDE-*life* uh-FISH-uhlz) people whose job is to study and protect wild animals

Bibliography

Feeney, Kathy. *Manatees.* Minnetonka, MN: NorthWord Press (2001).

Swinburne, Stephen R. *Saving Manatees.* Honesdale, PA: Boyds Mills Press (2006).

Thomas, Peggy. *Marine Mammal Preservation.* Brookfield, CT: Twenty-First Century Books (2000).

Walker, Sally M. *Manatees.* Minneapolis, MN: Carolrhoda Books (1999).

www.fws.gov/northflorida/

Read More

Lepthien, Emilie U. *Manatees.* Danbury, CT: Children's Press (1991).

Staub, Frank J. *Manatees.* Minneapolis, MN: Lerner Publications (1998).

Theodorou, Rod. *Florida Manatee (Animals in Danger).* Chicago: Heinemann Library (2001).

Learn More Online

To learn more about Florida manatees, visit
www.bearportpublishing.com/AnimalComebacks

Index

About the Author

Meish Goldish has written more than 100 books for children.
His book *Fossil Tales* won the Learning Magazine Teachers' Choice Award.